Our Befriending God

The Catholic Call to Holiness

Dennis J. Billy, C.Ss.R.

En Route Books and Media, LLC
Saint Louis, MO

En Route Books and Media, LLC
5705 Rhodes Avenue
St. Louis, MO 63109

Contact us at
contactus@enroutebooksandmedia.com

Cover Credit: Sebastian Mahfood

ISBN-13: 979-8-88870-542-1
Library of Congress Control Number:
Available online at https://catalog.loc.gov

For All My Lifelong Friends

This is my commandment, that you love one another as I have loved you. No one has greater love than this, to lay down one's life for one's friends.

John 15:12-13

Table of Contents

Introduction

What does it mean to be a saint? This book seeks to answer that question from within a Catholic outlook. We know that, over the centuries, the Catholic Church has officially canonized many saintly figures such as Saints Peter, Paul, Ignatius of Antioch, Irenaeus, Augustine, Anselm of Canterbury, Bernard of Clairvaux, Bonaventure, Thomas Aquinas, Catherine of Siena, Teresa of Avila, John of the Cross, Ignatius Loyola, Francis de Sales, Alphonsus de Liguori, John Vianney, Thérèse of Lisieux—to name but a few. Before doing so, she has thoroughly investigated and carefully scrutinized the lives, heroic virtues, and miracles attributed to these well-known saintly figures.

At the same time, we would be remiss to think that God has granted access to the beatific vision and heavenly glory only to this relatively small number, compared with the countless millions who have ever walked this earth. God, after all, wants everyone to be saved (1 Tm 2:4), and his grace is plentiful. More likely than not, the gates of heaven have been opened to many more holy souls than those listed on the

Church's liturgical calendar. The call to holiness is both penetrating and universal. Moreover, as Francis Thompson reminds us, Christ is a "hound of heaven" who pursues souls through the vicissitudes of this life and the purgation of the next.[1]

The Church, we must recall, is made up of the Church militant (the faithful on earth), the Church purgative (the faithful in purgatory), and the Church triumphant (the faithful in heaven). What holds them together is their faith in Christ (whether explicit or implicit), their hope of one day seeing God face to face, and the Holy Spirit, the soul of the Church, who dwells within them and guides them to their heavenly homeland through his holy promptings. The only ones to whom God refuses the beatific vision are those who refuse it themselves by the way they have lived their lives. In the end, a saint is a person who is a "friend of God," someone who has accepted his offer of friendship and allowed him to dwell in their heart by the gentle action of his Spirit.

---

[1] Francis Thompson, *The Hound of Heaven* in *Flowers of Heaven: One Thousand Years of Christian Verse*, ed. Joseph Pearce (San Francisco: Ignatius, 2005), 220-25.

This book has an Introduction, five chapters, and a conclusion. Chapter one, "The Catholic Vision," lays out the parameters of the Catholic outlook on reality. It places God at the center of all things, sees Christ as the fullness of God's revelation to humanity, and the Church and her sacraments as the primary means by which he extends his offer of friendship to each of us. Chapter two, "Our Journey Home," focuses on our end in God. It recognizes that we are strangers in a foreign land and must undergo a continuous process of purgation, illumination, and union to reach it. Chapter three, "The Call to Holiness," sees sanctity as being an intimate friend of God. It explores the various types of fear that mark our ongoing relationship with him and sees life in the Spirit as the ultimate expression of this friendship. Chapter four, "The Ways of Prayer," looks upon prayer as the great means of salvation. It considers the various kinds of prayer and proposes a new way of interpreting the call to pray without ceasing. Chapter five, "Following the Call," explores what hearing God's voice in the depths of our souls is like. It discusses how we can recognize his voice, acknowledge it, and follow it. Each chapter ends with a meditation on "Our Befriending God" and a prayer called "Talking with God." The Conclusion summarizes the book's findings and ends with an encouragement to the reader to take them to heart.

This book seeks to delve more deeply into what it means to walk the path of holiness. It claims not to exhaust so rich a topic but hopes merely to whet the reader's appetite. Its most salient insight is that each person's relationship with God is unique in all the world and meant to reflect his glory in a particular way. It hopes to kindle a thirst for God in those who read and ponder its pages, and encourages those who do so to converse with God as they would a friend, tell him what is in their mind and heart, listen to his still small voice, and follow it wherever it goes, and without counting the cost.

Chapter One

The Catholic Vision

Catholicism provides a comprehensive and cohesive vision of existence and all that flows from it. This vision supports everything Catholicism stands for. Without it, all Catholic doctrine and ethical teaching collapses from within. With it, we have an unrivaled explanation of the world, all it holds, and whatever lies beyond it. In this first chapter, we will examine the contours of this vision and its significance for the Catholic call to holiness.

Before the Beginning

Catholicism maintains that God is Love and that Love underpins all of reality. God is Existence itself and embodies the transcendental values of the One, the True, the Good, and the Beautiful. God created all that exists, which shares ("participates") in his Existence, and was designed to espouse the values that flow from him. God's Oneness is not static but dynamic. His Oneness stems from an eternal sharing of interpersonal Love that manifests itself in Three Divine Persons in One God. The dogma of the Blessed Trinity resolves the perennial philosophical problem of the One and the Many by juxtaposing the Greek concept of divine immutability with the Hebrew concept of a personal God who enters into covenant with his people. When seen in this light, God is Three Persons in One God: God the Father, Eternally Transcendent; God the Son, Eternally Begotten by the Father; and God the Holy Spirit, Eternally Proceeding from the Father and the Son. This intimate community of Love exists beyond time and space, since it is the Creator of time and space, and of everything within and beyond them. Because God is Love, he is Eternally Free. He is bound by nothing except his own divine nature and the values inherent in it.

In the Beginning

"In the beginning was the Word, and the Word was with God, and the Word was God" (Jn 1:1).[1]

[1] Unless otherwise states, all Scripture quotations come from *Holy Bible: New Revised Standard Version with Apocrypha* (New York: Oxford University Press, 1989).

According to Catholic belief, there are three great divine actions: Creation, Redemption, and Sanctification. Although God always acts as one, each of these actions is associated with one of the Persons of the Trinity: Creation with the Father, Redemption with the Son, and Sanctification with the Holy Spirit. Because God exists outside of time, he knew the consequences of his actions and decided to act despite them. In the beginning, he created the world and everything in it, knowing all along that humanity would choose to follow its own will and fall from grace. He made us *capax Dei* ("capable of God"), creating us in his own image and likeness so that we could freely choose to return his love and enter into an intimate friendship with him. When seen in this light, God's creative activity already contained the seeds of his redemptive love and sanctifying grace. He foresaw our inherent weakness and acted to give himself to us completely by entering our world, becoming one of us, nourishing us with his body and blood, and enkindling a hope that we would one day see him face to face. Athanasius of Alexandria (d. 373) says it best, "God became man so man might become divine."[2]

God created the world out of freedom (not from necessity) because his love is self-diffusive and seeks to share itself with others. He fashioned the world so that he could people it with beings created in his own image and capable of returning that love. To do so, he had to give us free will, which, by its very nature, included the possibility of not returning his love by choosing to disobey his commands so we could grow apart from him and go our own way. As the *Catechism of the Catholic* Church points out, "The account of the fall in Genesis 3 uses figurative language, but affirms a primeval event, a deed that took place *at the beginning of the history of man*."[3] This original fall from grace had consequences not just for humanity but for all creation. For us, it meant that our minds had become darkened, our wills weakened, our internal senses of memory and imagination enfeebled, and our emotions disordered and out of sync with one another and with our higher rational powers. It

---

[2]Athanasius of Alexandria, *On the Incarnation,* 54.3.

[3] *Catechism of the Catholic Church*, no. 390.

also meant that our bodies would become susceptible to illness and disease, and we would face an aging process and the reality of death with fear and trembling. As the Apostle Paul remarks, "...just as sin came into the world through one man, and death came through sin, and so death spread to all because all have sinned" (Rom 5:12). For the rest of creation, it meant that a perfectly ordered world would be deeply wounded from within and left in serious disarray. The garden created by God would be corrupted from within and preyed upon by the world's evil forces, as represented by the serpent's cunning in the story of the Fall.

Jesus, we are told, is "...the Alpha and Omega, the beginning and the end" (Rev 21:6). All things have their origins and final consummation in him. He was present at the world's creation and is the source of its final transformation in the New Creation. He is "the image of the invisible God, the firstborn of all creation" (Col 1:15). What is more, "He himself is before all things, and in him all things hold together. He is the head of the body, the church; he is the beginning, the firstborn from the dead, so that he might come to have first place in everything" (Col 17-18). Jesus of

Nazareth is the Christ, the Redeemer of the world. In him and through him, our wounded world and all things in it (especially we ourselves, the pinnacle of God's creation) are being healed of its mortal infirmities and transformed by his kenotic self-emptying on the cross of wood. He is the Lamb of God who takes away the sins of the world. We have been washed in the blood of the Lamb, sanctified by his Holy Spirit, who came to us at Pentecost and who promises to accompany us on our journey through life.

The New Man

God created the world, redeemed it when it went awry, transformed it, and continues to do so to this very day through the vivifying presence of his Spirit. Jesus defeated Death by the blood of the cross and rose from the dead on the third day with a glorified humanity that he now shares with us as members of his body, the Church. The blood and water that soaked the ground when it flowed from his side at Golgotha initiated the New Creation that would rise from the ashes of the Old. Jesus, the New Man, is a corporate reality, something unknown to us until the coming of Christ. The Apostle Paul says it best: "For just as the body is one and has many members, and all the members of the body, though many, are one body, so it is with Christ. For in the one Spirit we were all baptized into one body—Jews or Greeks, slaves or free—we were all made to drink of one Spirit' (1 Cor 12:12-13). Paul's imagery of the body is more than a simple metaphor. Rather, it points to a corporate ontological reality that we share by virtue of our being immersed in Christ's paschal mystery at baptism and, through him and in him, have been made adopted sons and daughters of the Father. The Holy Spirit is the soul of this corporate reality and enables us to share in the intimate love of the Triune God. Jesus himself once told his disciples, "No one has greater love than this, to lay down one's life for one's friends. You are my friends if you do what I command you" (Jn 15:13-14). His commandment to us is quite clear, "This is my commandment, that you love one another as I have loved you" (Jn 15: 12). This is the mark of a true disciple. The bare truth of it all is that we cannot live this way without the help of the Spirit.

The Holy Spirit, also known as the Advocate, the Paraclete, and the Comforter, descended upon the nascent community of believers on the feast of Pentecost, fifty days after the resurrection and ten days after Christ's ascension into heaven. That event marks the birthday of the Church, the Mystical Body of Christ, and its march down the corridors of time to fulfill Christ's commission to his disciples, "Go therefore and make disciples of all nations, baptizing them in the name of the Father and of the Son and of the Holy Spirit" (Mt 28: 19). He promised to be with them always even to the end of time (Mt 28: 20). He does so primarily through the gift of his Spirit, who vivifies his Church by his presence. Jesus himself said that he must leave this world so he could be present to his followers in a new and dynamic way: "It is to your advantage that I go away, for if I do not go, the Advocate will not come to you; but if I go, I will send him to you" (Jn 16: 7). By the gift of his Spirit, Jesus can dwell in our hearts and befriend each of us in a very intimate and personal way. In one sense, it is a continuation of the mystery of the Incarnation. Jesus entered our world some 2,000 years ago. Now he wishes to enter each of our own inner worlds and continue this redeeming action through the sanctifying and transforming work of his Spirit. The Spirit, in other words, seeks to take possession of our souls. He does so, however, not by controlling us like a puppet on a string (as the Evil One would have it), but by enabling us to become our deepest, truest selves by living within us and bestowing upon us his manifold gifts and fruits.

Life in the Spirit goes beyond our wildest dreams. God loves us so much that he shares himself with us and, in doing so, divinizes us, enabling us to share in the intimate love of the Trinity. What is more, Christ's corporate, divinized body, the Church, is now making its way through history. The Spirit is present to her in a special way through the authority of the magisterium (that is, the college of bishops in communion with the successor of Peter) to guide her on this journey with inspired teaching, by correctly interpreting the truths of revelation in Scripture and Tradition, and most especially through the sacraments, which "...are perceptible signs (words and actions) accessible to our human nature. By the action of Christ and the power of the Holy Spirit, they make present efficaciously the grace that they signify."[4]

---

[4] Ibid., no. 1084.

Christ, we might say, is the sacrament of God; the Church, the sacrament of Christ; and the sacraments, those of the Church. The sacraments are actions of Christ and are just as real as the miracles and actions he performed when he walked this earth. The Eucharist, moreover, "the source and summit of the Christian life,"[5] is even more than an action of Christ, for it not only immerses us in the mystery of his passion, death, and ascension into heaven, but gives us Christ himself, his own body and blood present in the consecrated bread and wine, to eat and drink for our spiritual nourishment. As Jesus himself one said, "Verily truly, I tell you, unless you eat the flesh of the Son of Man and drink his blood, you have no life in you" (Jn 6:53). Unlike earthly food that we digest and make a part of ourselves, this heavenly food, "the bread of angels," works in reverse: it transforms us so we can share in Jesus' divinized humanity. Through the Eucharist, Christ's Mystical Body is nourished by his resurrected and glorified humanity, thereby enabling it to glorify God the Father. As it says in the memorial acclamation of the Mass: "Through him, and with

---

[5] Second Vatican Council, *Lumen gentium*, no. 11.

him, and in him, O God, almighty Father, in the unity of the Holy Spirit, all glory and honor is yours, for ever and ever."[6] The point here is that Christ himself, the head of the Church, is transforming the members of his body from the inside out. He walks ahead of us to guide us, behind us to catch us when we fall, beside us to accompany us on our journey, and within us to befriend us, transform us, and dwell within our hearts. What is more, Mary, Jesus' mother, is not only the Mother of God, but also the Mother of the Church and all the faithful. She provides a sense of warmth, tenderness, and belonging to the faithful throughout their spiritual sojourn and beyond. She is Jesus' first and closest disciple and wishes nothing more than to draw others closer to her Son. As the *Salve Regina* tells us, she is "our life, our sweetness, and our hope." At the end of her earthly sojourn, she was assumed body and soul into heaven and is the only one of the faithful who has experienced the fullness of redemption. Everyone else is awaiting the resurrection of their bodies at the end of time, while she

---

[6] *The Roman Missal*, (Magnificat, 2011), 633.

sits at the right hand of her Son at this very moment as Queen of Heaven.

Christ's Redeeming Action

Christ loves us so much that he also allows us to share in his redeeming action. As members of his Mystical Body, we are immersed in his Paschal Mystery and participate in the salvific passion, death, resurrection, and ascension into heaven. This is possible because his death on Golgotha and the events that followed occurred both in and out of time. His passion, death, and resurrection were all historical, transhistorical, and transcendent: in the here and now, yet also extending across history and into the beyond. When seen in this light, his Paschal Mystery is not unlike the Incarnation. Just as the transcendent God entered our world and became one of us in the person of Jesus of Nazareth, so too was his death on the cross lifted into the transcendent mystery of the divine, becoming something beyond death.

How do we share in Christ's paschal mystery? As members of his Mystical Body, we seek to live as Christ lived. We open our hearts and minds to his

Spirit and allow him to transform us by dwelling within us and filling us with his myriad gifts and fruits. "Grace perfects nature," as the saying goes.[7] When we allow the Spirit into our lives, we begin to think, feel, and act as Christ did when he walked this earth some 2,000 years ago, and as he does now. Jesus told his disciples how they should act. He narrowed the 613 laws of the Jewish Torah down to two: "You shall love the Lord your God with all your heart, and with all your soul, and with all your mind' and "You shall love your neighbor as yourself." (Mt 22:37-40). These two commandments are found, respectively, in Deuteronomy (6:5) and Leviticus (19:18), and they summarize everything contained in the Law and the prophets. The problem for us is that we cannot fulfill even these commandments on our own. We need God's help. It is only by the power of the Holy Spirit dwelling within us that we can act in this way. Acting in this way, moreover, helps shape our inner selves and gradually transforms us into the persons God envisions us to become.

---

[7] Thomas Aquinas, *Summa theologiae*, I, q. 1, a. 8, ad 2m.

To be more specific, in baptism we are immersed in Christ's Paschal Mystery and become adopted sons and daughters of the Father. In Confirmation, we affirm our faith in the Lord and are blessed with the seven gifts of the Holy Spirit: wisdom, understanding, counsel, knowledge, fortitude, piety, and fear of the Lord. These gifts build into the infused virtues of faith, hope, and charity, as well as the cardinal virtues of prudence, justice, fortitude, and temperance, which have themselves already been transformed by the grace of the Spirit. The gift of wisdom perfects charity; knowledge and understanding perfect faith; fear of the Lord perfects hope; counsel perfects prudence; piety perfects justice; fortitude perfects courage; and fear of the Lord perfects temperance.[8] Through these gifts, the Spirit takes over in our lives and yet does so in a way that enables us to become our truest, deepest selves. By responding to the promptings of the Spirit, we can fulfill Jesus' commandments of love and, as a result, the myriad fruits of the Spirit pour out from us: "love, joy, peace,

---

[8] See Servais Pinckaers, *The Sources of Christian Ethics*, trans. Mary Rhomas Noble (Washington, D.C.: The Catholic University of America Press, 1995), 179.

patience, kindness, generosity faithfulness, gentleness and self-control" (Gal 5: 22-23). These qualities of the Spirit are those of Jesus himself. The Spirit dwelling within us is the New Law, the Evangelical Law, the Law of the Gospel.[9] When we live in the Spirit, we begin to think, will, remember, imagine, feel, and act as Jesus did. With his Spirit dwelling within us, we are gradually conformed unto his mind and heart. He is "the way, and the truth, and the life" (Jn 14:6). In him and through his blood, we have been redeemed. By living in his Spirit, his redemptive love continues to heal wounded hearts and transform them down the corridors of time.

As stated earlier, God always acts as one, although each of his divine actions is typically associated with one of the Persons in the Blessed Trinity. Through the Father, God created, is creating, and continues to create. Through the Son, he redeemed, is redeeming, and continues to redeem. Through the Spirit, he sanctified, is sanctifying, and continues to sanctify. He does so to this very day through the Church and her sacraments, and especially through the members of his

---

[9] Thomas Aquinas, *Summa theologiae*, qq. 106-8.

Mystical Body, all of whom share, in varying degrees, in his glorified humanity. We are all on a spiritual journey. The threefold way of purgation, illumination, and union applies to every one of us. The Church is made up of those still here on earth (Church militant), those who have died yet are still making their way to the Lord (Church purgative), and those who have arrived at the end of their journey (Church triumphant). God wishes everyone to be saved (2 Tm 2:3-4) and, through his Spirit, calls each of us by name and gently draws us to himself. Our job is not to place any obstacles in the way and, for this very reason, we must ask the Lord to help us to be faithful to our calling until our journey's end.

Conclusion

The Catholic vision of reality places God at the center of all things. He is Existence itself and created the universe and everything in it. Because he is Love, he wishes to diffuse himself as much as possible by sharing himself with others. For this reason, he must have a communal dimension to his nature. The Catholic dogma of the Trinity resolves the philosophical problem of the One and the Many by affirming that God has one divine nature composed of three divine Persons: Father, Son, and Spirit. This intimate community of Love lies at the root of all reality. Everything that exists (including Time and Space themselves) merely participates in God's existence and does so by God's will. God is One, True, Good, and Beautiful. All that exists is ontologically good and was created as such. Because God wanted creatures who could reciprocate his love, he gave human beings, the pinnacle of his creation, free will, enabling them to return his love or reject it. The evil in the world stems from humanity's choice at the dawn of time to rebel against God and go its own way. This sin of human origins, what the Church calls "original sin," has had ripple effects throughout creation.

There are three primary divine actions: Creation, Redemption, and Sanctification. Although God always acts as one, each of these actions is typically associated with one of the divine Persons of the Triune God: Creation with the Father, Redemption with the Son, and Sanctification with the Holy Spirit. Because of Adam's sin at the dawn of time, humanity and all creation fell from their pristine state and have become deeply wounded. Because of this, God's redemptive action went into effect. God entered our world in the person of Jesus Christ and redeemed it through his passion, death, and resurrection. He ascended into heaven so that he could send us his Spirit to dwell in our hearts, sanctify us, and ultimately transform us by allowing us to share in his glorified humanity.

God continues his creative, redemptive, and sanctifying mission through the Church and her sacraments, which are actions of Christ's Mystical Body. As members of that Body, with Christ our Head and Mary our Mother, we, the faithful, share in these divine actions. Christ, in other words, continues his redemptive mission through the indwelling of the Spirit, who lives and acts in and through us. Christ continues to live in the members of his body and, through them, continues his redeeming and sanctifying mission down the corridors of time. This Catholic vision of reality places Christ at the center of history. He is the Alpha and Omega, the Beginning and the End: "In him we live and move and have our being" (Acts 17:28).

Our Befriending God

God loves us so much that he decided to enter our world to heal it of its wounds and transform it. He wishes to do the same in us. He will not do so, however, against our will. To receive him into our hearts, we must freely choose to embrace his offer of friendship and reciprocate his love. He created us for this very reason. The whole of creation exists for the purpose of enabling us to share in the intimate love of Father, Son, and Holy Spirit. We were created to share in God's intimate community of love. He gives us the freedom to receive his love or reject it and go our own way.

Talking with God

Dear Lord, I believe in you and wish to establish a friendship with you. I believe that this desire is itself a blessing. Help me open my heart to you. Help me to invite you into every nook and cranny of my soul, especially in those places that are dark and lonely. Come, Lord Jesus, come! I love you and would like you to dwell in my heart. Teach me the ways of friendship. Help me become one of your closest friends.

Chapter Two

Our Journey Home

The Catholic vision understands life on earth as a journey and our actions in this world as determining our final destiny. God wants everyone to spend eternity in his presence, but because he has given us free will, he allows us to choose whether to do so. Unlike the Evil One, who wishes to control us like puppets on a string, he wants us to come to him of our own accord. When we cooperate with his grace, our actions will help us find our way to him. If we do not, we will live forever closed in upon ourselves and left to our own resources. As C. S. (1898-1963) once said, "The doors of hell are locked from the inside."[1] In this chapter, we will look at the contours of our earthly journey and what we must bring with us along the way.

---

[1] C.S. Lewis, *The Problem of Pain* (New York: Macmillan,1962), 127.

Strangers in a Foreign Land

Most Catholics are familiar with the words "parish" and "parochial." Most of us belong to a parish, and many of us have attended parochial (or "parish") schools. The origin of these terms tells us something about our journey through life, for they come from the Greek word *paroikia*, which means "stranger in a foreign land" or "sojourner." The very way Catholics organize their lives on earth indicates the temporary nature of their passage through life.

As St. Augustine of Hippo (354-430) states in his *City of God*, we go through this life with one foot in the City of Man and another in the City of God.[2] There is an eschatological (already-but-not-yet) quality to this earthly sojourn. In one sense, we are on the road and have not yet arrived at our final destiny; in another, we already have a heavenly foretaste of it in the sacraments and the Word of God. After all, before he ascended to heaven, Jesus himself said to his disciples, "I am with you always, to the end of the age" (Mt 28:20).

---

[2] Augustine of Hippo, *City of God*, 16.28.

In addition to his presence in the Church, his Word, and the seven sacraments, Jesus is present to us through the indwelling of his Spirit in our hearts, where he befriends us and reveals to us the ways of holiness. In this way, he can be present to each of us in a way that could never have happened had he chosen not to ascend to the right hand of his Father in heaven. He is especially present to us in the Eucharist, which makes present in an unbloody way his sacrifice on the cross on Golgotha. Jesus rose from the dead some 2,000 years ago but now seeks to rise within our hearts and incorporate us into his glorified humanity.

On the Road

There are many types of journeys: a trip to the local grocery store, a single day from dusk to dawn, a pilgrimage to Rome, Santiago de Compostela, or the Holy Land. Life itself can be considered a journey. Some people will say that life is a journey: you are born, you live, and you die. For them, nothing lies beyond the pale of death. Catholics see it differently. We believe in life after death. Life is but a preparation for what lies after death. How we live our lives will indicate what comes afterward. Our journey through life is a spiritual one. As St. Paul reminds us, "…we walk by faith, not by sight" (2 Cor 5:7).

As with any journey, our earthly sojourn has a beginning, a middle, and an end. No one would begin a journey if they thought its end or goal did not exist. Similarly, we would not set out to seek our heavenly destiny if we did not believe in God and could one day see him face to face. What is more, we would not set out on a journey if we did not live in the hope of one day getting there. So too, our earthly sojourn must be enlivened by the hope that our efforts will bear fruit and lead us, one day, to our end in God. Finally, each journey takes place in stages. There are also the planning, execution, and arrival stages (what we do when we get there). For Catholics, that means that our journey must be carefully planned and executed in love. As St. Paul reminds us, "And now faith, hope, and love abide, these three; and the greatest of these is love" (1 Cor 13:13).

These three theological virtues are fueled by prayer, which is like breathing to any journey. We cannot journey on a single breath, but must do it constantly, at all times. Jesus himself taught his disciples the importance of praying at all times and not to lose heart (Lk 18:1), while St. Paul encourages the Thessalonians thus: "Rejoice always, pray without ceasing, give thanks in all circumstances; for this is the will of God in Christ Jesus for you" (1 Thes 5:16-18). Without prayer, these virtues begin to decompose. As St. Alphonsus de Liguori (1696-1787) reminds us, "...the grace of prayer is given to everyone."[3]

Prayer presupposes faith and strengthens it. Faith, in turn, gives rise to hope, and hope gives rise to love. When we stop praying, we cease to love, lose hope, and ultimately become devoid of faith. The opposite of faith is unbelief, that is, refusing to accept a clearly recognized truth. The opposite of hope is, on the one hand, despair and, on the other, presumption. The opposites of love are hatred and indifference. The Catholic journey is one of faith, hope, and love; it is fueled by prayer and life in the Spirit, who dwells. Within our hearts, and manifests in us his myriad gifts and fruits.

---

[3] Alphonsus de Liguori, *Prayer, The Great Means of Salvation*, 1.2.4.

The Threefold Journey

Our spiritual journey is often depicted as unfolding in three stages: the purgative, the illuminative, and the unitive.[4] These, in turn, are sometimes described as the beginning, intermediate, and final phases of the spiritual life. They are sometimes viewed linearly, as if one follows another successively and leaves the other behind. Another view is that they appear regularly in our lives in a more circular fashion. When seen in this light, we would experience during our lifetime. various cycles of purgation, illumination, and union. We can model their relationship as an upward-spiraling motion of increasingly small cycles until they ultimately reach a single point of perfect union with God. With this in mind, let us look at the contours of each stage and consider its role in the spiritual life.

The Way of Purgation. This stage recognizes the need for detachment in our lives. Much of life is about letting go. As we journey through life, we tend to hold

---

[4] See, for example, Pseudo-Dionysius, *On Divine Names*, 4.9; *The Ecclesiastical Hierarchy*, 6.3.

onto things for a variety of reasons: pleasure, power, possessions. If we are not careful, these worldly attachments can weaken our reliance on God and even eliminate it. If we are to focus on our ultimate end, we need to put these worldly attachments in their proper perspective. The goods of the world need not interfere with our relationship with God. Given our weakened natures, however, they can easily get in the way and even completely obstruct our relationship with him. A saying attributed to St. Alphonsus de Liguori (1696-1787) goes like this: "You cannot fill a crystal vase with light if it is filled with dirt." Similarly, the soul cannot be filled with the graces of the Holy Spirit if it is full of unnecessary worldly attachments that dull its sense of the transcendent and its need for God. Prayer, fasting, and almsgiving are the traditional means given us by God to weaken such attachments, let go of them, and ultimately be free to cling to the Spirit and follow God's commands.

The Illuminative Way. As we purify ourselves of undue attachments, the light of the Spirit gradually enters our souls. Although it can happen in an instant, it normally occurs gradually and helps us sense the Spirit working within us and respond to his promptings. As this process unfolds, we experience a deepening of our understanding of the faith in both mind and heart. The Spirit desires to occupy every corner of our souls. The more he enters within us, the easier it is for us to sense his presence both within ourselves, in those around us, and in all creation. The illuminative way enables us not only to keep God's commandments, but also to grow in the life of virtue. As we follow this path, we experience a deepening of the theological virtues of faith, hope, and love in our lives, and the natural virtues of prudence, justice, fortitude, and temperance become infused with grace and oriented toward God as their end. As we proceed along the illuminative way, we find that the need for purgation, while always there, becomes less. Detachment from worldly things gives way to attachment to God. Our minds and hearts gradually become filled with divine light, preparing us for the way of union.

The Unitive Way. As purgation leads to illumination, illumination leads to union. This stage of the spiritual life follows the previous two. As stated previously, these stages do not follow linearly, as if one is completely left behind before proceeding to the next, but rather in an upward-spiraling motion that ultimately leads to a single point of complete and utter union with the divine. This latter stage fills the entire soul and manifests itself in a complete uniformity of wills. When seen in this light, the spiritual life may be said to be a movement from non-conformity with God's will (purgative stage) to conformity with God's will (illuminative stage) to a complete uniformity with God's will (unitive stage). The difference between conformity and uniformity with God's will is that in the former, one still experiences one's will as being distinct from God's. In contrast, in the latter, one experiences no difference. Of course, the distinction between creature and Creator always remains, but in the unitive stage, we see no difference between our will and God's. In this mystical stage of union, the Spirit wishes to enter every dimension of our being: the intellect, the will, the internal senses of memory and imagination, the five exterior senses, and ultimately union with God himself. Although God blesses some with this unitive experience in this life, most of us will not be blessed with this final stage of union, and we must wait for it in the life to come. Be that as it may, God wishes us all to enter into the divine friendship.

Friends of God

We embark on this spiritual journey to become intimate friends with God. God entered our world and became one of us for this very reason. He created us with free will so we could reciprocate his love and become one with him. What Jesus said to his disciples, he now says to us: "I do not call you servants any longer, because the servant does not know what the master is doing; but I have called you friends, because I have made known to you everything that I have heard from my Father" (Jn 15:15).

In his book, *The Four Loves*, C.S. Lewis (1898-1963) distinguishes friendship (*philia*) from three other types of love: human affection (*storge*), romantic love (*eros*), and selfless love (*agape*).[5] Natural human affection is the love a parent has for a son or daughter. Romantic love is when two people stare into each other's eyes, fall in love, and are overtaken by a kind of madness. Selfless love always has no favorites and places others before oneself. Friendship

---

[5] C. S. Lewis, *The Four Loves* (San Diego: Harvest, 1960), 87-127.

differs from these other loves in that it involves a bond between two individuals based on a common interest. Rather than staring into each other's eyes, as in romantic love, they draw close by virtue of their love for something outside of themselves. Some Christians, like Søren Kierkegaard and Anders Nygren, have pitted friendship against agape because they thought it was exclusive.[6] A closer look at friendship, however, reveals that when friendship is rooted in Christ, it expands in ever-increasing circles and is not, in fact, opposed to *agape*, but deepens it.

In his *Nicomachean Ethics*, Aristotle (384-322 BC) discusses friendship at length.[7] He says there are different kinds of friendship: those of pleasure, utility, and character. We can befriend someone because we enjoy their presence, they are useful to us, or they help us grow in virtue. Although each of these can be genuine to a certain extent, he says that friendships of character are the deepest and truest form of friendship, because each friend seeks to help the other

---

[6] See Paul J. Wadell, *Friendship and the Moral Life* (Note Dame, IN: University of Notre Dame Press, 1989), 74-96.

[7] Aristotle, *Nicomachean Ethics*, Bks 8-9.

become more virtuous. In friendships of character, he identifies three primary marks or qualities: benevolence, reciprocity, and mutual indwelling. Benevolence means wishing the other person well and actively seeking their well-being. Reciprocity refers to the importance of friendship being mutual and not forced on another. Mutual indwelling refers to the experience of true friends sharing their hearts and experiencing a deep sense of intimacy and closeness.

In his *Summa theologiae*, Thomas Aquinas (d. 1274) summarizes Aristotle's notion of the marks of friendship and goes on to describe charity *(agape)* as "the friendship of man for God."[8] Our friendship with Christ, the Incarnate Word of God and Son of the Father, enables us to enter into friendship with the Father and the intimate love of the Blessed Trinity. Because of this friendship, the Holy Spirit dwells within our hearts and, through him, we dwell in the heart of both Father and Son. Jesus himself once said, "The Father and I are one" (Jn 10:30). Friendship with Christ enables us to become friends of the Father, and also friends of one another. We who are sojourners,

---

[8] Thomas Aquinas, *Summa theologiae*, II-II, q. 23, a. 1, resp.

"strangers in a foreign land," are making our way to the other side of death, beyond the empty tomb, to join Jesus, his Mother, Mary, and all the saints in what Mr. Blue calls "the tavern at the end of the world."

> When the day comes that the sky is emptied of stars, and the sun is black, and the distraught winds have only the void for their lament, I am sure that somewhere I will be merry together, somewhere good hearts will greet good hearts, and somewhere our dreams of unbroken love and good talk and laughter will have come true. This is a glorious Somewhere, and it is far nearer to us than the stars. There, Our Lady talks of children to unknown mothers who taught their many children the love of her single Son. There, Saint Joseph is a man among peasants. There Xavier is home from his wars, and there Suarez and Aquinas have their arguments out. There, Thomas More swaps jests with the older Teresa, while the younger Teresa gathers her roses. There, Saint George boasts of his conquest of the dragon, and mayhap the

> Good Thief listens, or mayhap he hears little Saint Francis singing his songs. It is a good place, this Somewhere. It has been called Paradise. It has been called the Tavern at the End of the World. And it has been called Home. It is only Catholicism that would ever allow the likes of me to hope someday to be there.[9]

The saints of old were known as the "friends of God."[10] They were called such because of their holy lives and closeness to God. We, too, are called to holiness. We are also called to be "friends of God."

The Unending Journey

Good friends like to be together; they enjoy one another's company. Because we can become friends with God during our earthly sojourn, we can say that, even now, we have a foretaste of what heaven will be like. The eschatological (already-but-not-yet) nature

---

[9] Myles Connolly, *Mr. Blue* (Garden City, NY: Image Books, 1928), 36-37.

[10] Peter Brown, *The Making of Late Antiquity* (Cambridge, MA: Harvard University Press, 1978), 54-80.

of friendship with God sheds light on a saying attributed to St. Catherine of Siena (1347-80), "All the way to heaven is heaven, because Jesus said, 'I am the Way.'" We spend so much time thinking of heaven as the end of our journey that we sometimes forget we have a foretaste of it even along the way. As the Redemptorist motto reminds us, "With him is plentiful redemption." Heaven, in other words, is our end, but also so much more than that. It is not a static place where we float around on clouds in endless boredom, but a deep sharing in the life of the Trinity, which begins even during our earthly sojourn.

To share in the intimate life of God, moreover, means that we also share in the divine actions. God, as we have seen, always acts as one. Still, each of his divine actions is generally associated with one of the three Persons: Creation (with the Father), Redemption (with the Son), and Sanctification (with the Holy Spirit). God loves us so much that he wants us not only to share in his inner life but also in his divine actions. That is to say that we will share in his creative, redemptive, and sanctifying activity and do so for all eternity.

What is more, God will dwell in *our* hearts and share in *our* activities. St. Alphonsus de Liguori once said, "The paradise of God…is the heart of man."[11] This mutual indwelling of hearts points to what heaven will be like once we pass beyond the pale of death, are purified, enlightened, and finally united in complete uniformity with his will. In his *Life of Moses*, St. Gregory of Nyssa (c. 335-c. 394) reminds us that our journey into God will never end. He calls it *epektasis,* an eternal journey into the mystery of God's love.[12] Because God's heart is infinite and ours finite, we will never be able to grasp the infinite extent of his heart and mind fully. Amid eternal bliss, there will always be something else to discover.

Conclusion

We are all sojourners, strangers in a foreign land. That journey will lead to the presence of God or an eternal life without him, which could be described as nothing more than a living hell. On this journey,

---

[11] Alphonsus de Liguori, *The Way to Converse Always and Familiarly with God*, 1.

[12] Gregory of Nyssa, *The Life of Moses*, 2.239.

Jesus goes before us to guide us, behind us to catch us when we fall, beside us to accompany us, and within us to befriend us. God created us because he wanted creatures who could freely reciprocate his love or freely reject it.

Faith, hope, and love, the three things that last, are necessary for this journey. Each of them requires God's grace and our heartfelt cooperation. Our spiritual journey requires the belief that heaven, our ultimate end, exists; the hope that one day we will get there; and the necessary acts of love that will, step by step, day by day, lead us to our journey's end. Along the journey, we must detach ourselves from worldly desires so that we can be filled with the light of the Spirit, and unite our wills completely with God's. Although some of us will experience God mystically in this life, all who pray and cooperate with the Spirit's grace will be saved and one day see him face to face in the beatific vision.

That vision will forever grow ever deeper. What we see as we journey into the mystery of God will become ever clearer and more focused. At the same time, there will always be something more of him to see, something more of him to discover. If "paradise for God… is the heart of man," then heaven for us is a never-ending journey into the mystery of the divine. We will never be able to fully exhaust the mystery of God. He created us in his image and likeness so that he could share his love with us for all eternity. The destiny of the saints, the "friends of God," is to travel into the mystery of God, who has revealed himself to us in Christ Jesus, bequeathed to us his Spirit, and yet remains to us, at the same time, both intimately known and eternally unknown.

Our Befriending God

Do you consider yourself a pilgrim, a "stranger in a foreign land"? Do you view your Life as a journey? If so, where did it begin, and how will it end? Do you believe that Life continues after Death? If so, how does that change your attitude toward Life itself? What do the virtues of faith, hope, and love have to do with your journey? What about prayer? What about the threefold way of purgation, illumination, and union? Do you think about this journey often? Seldom? Not at all? What can you do to make your journey through Life easier? What burdens are you carrying? What will it take to let them go?

Talking with God

Dear Lord, I know that I have taken some wrong turns in my journey through Life. I believe my Life is meant to end with you, being in your presence, and seeing you face to face. Help me get back on track. Help me let go of the things that lead me astray. Help me to always keep my eyes on you. I am sorry for the times I have focused too much on myself and forgotten all about you. Fill my mind with thoughts of you. Help me each day, one step at a time. Let me never be separated from you again.

Chapter Three

The Call to Holiness

The Catholic faith is all about the call to holiness. God wishes that everyone be saved (1 Tm 2:4-6) and live in a deep, personal, and intimate relationship with him. He wants to befriend every one of us, no matter how long it takes. As we have seen, many of us will spend our entire lives trying to deepen our relationship with him. The only thing that can hinder this process is our own refusal to enter into friendship with him. As we have also seen, friendship is a two-way street. It must be reciprocal. We return God's love for us by keeping his commandments. As Jesus himself once said, "If you love me, you will keep my commandments" (Jn 14:15). Many more of us will require a time of purgation even after we die. What is more, because God is infinite and we are not, the journey into the mystery of friendship with him will never end. There will always be something more for us to discover about him. In this chapter, we will look at the call to holiness and the various ways we respond to it.

Called to Be One

The call to holiness comes through most clearly in Jesus' prayer to the Father in the Gospel of John: "Sanctify them in the truth; your word is truth. As you have sent me into the world, so I have sent them into the world. And for their sakes I sanctify myself, so that they also may be sanctified I truth" (Jn 21: 17-19). He goes on: "I ask not only on behalf of these, but also on behalf of those who will believe in me through their word, that they may all be one. As you, Father, are in me and I am in you, may they also be in us, so that the world may believe that you have sent me" (Jn 21: 20-21).

We can infer several things about holiness from these verses. First of all, holiness is rooted in truth, and that truth is rooted in God's Word. Since Jesus himself is the Word of God, holiness means being rooted in a personal relationship with him. We can enter into a relationship with him by opening our hearts and inviting him to enter and dwell there, so that we can keep his commandments. We cannot keep them without his help. If we try to do so, we are doomed to fail. Jesus also simplified the 613 commandments in the Torah to two. When asked which was the greatest of the commandments, he replied: "'You shall love the Lord your God with all your heart, and with all your soul, and with all your mind.' This is the greatest and first commandment. And a second is like it: 'You shall love your neighbor as yourself.' On these two commandments hang all the law and the prophets" (Mt 22:37-40). The first of these commandments comes from the Book of Deuteronomy (Dt 6:5) and the second from the Book of Leviticus (Lv 19:18). Unlike the Pharisees, who multiplied the demands of the Torah, Jesus narrowed them to two. Elsewhere, he goes on further by giving his disciples a new commandment: "I give you a new commandment, that you love one another. Just as I have loved you, you also should love one another. By this everyone will know that you are my disciples, if you have love for one another" (Jn 13:34-35). Jesus, in other words, is the fulfillment of the Law and Prophets. We know we are rooted in the truth if we are rooted in him and love as he loves.

Being one with Jesus and his heavenly Father, however, does not erase the Creator/creature distinction. Being one with him does not mean that we lose our creaturely status and are somehow absorbed into the Godhead. Holiness means that we share in Christ's divinized humanity and thus share in the divine love, while maintaining our unique creaturely identities. If holiness refers to the indwelling of the Holy Spirit, it does not mean that the Spirit, who is Uncreated Grace, actually lives in our hearts without some divine mediation. If that were so, our finite humanity would not be able to bear the weight of God's infinite divinity. Rather, it is by created grace, or what Eastern Christians call the "divine energies," that we share in Christ's divinized humanity and come to share in the divine love. God's love, in other words, is both freely given and self-diffusive. He created us in his image and likeness and made us *capax Dei* ("capable of God") so that he could share his divine life with his creatures and, through us, the rest of creation.

Fearing the Lord

If holiness is rooted in truth, and if Jesus is "the way, and the truth, and the life" (Jn 14:6), and if keeping his commandments is an indication of true discipleship, then we must also look at the motivations behind our desire to follow his will and to love one another as he has loved us. One way of doing so is to look at the various types of "fear of the Lord" that lead us to follow his will: servile fear, mixed fear, filial fear, and the Spirit's gift of "fear of the Lord."[1] Let us look at each of these in due order.

Servile fear is the fear of punishment. We strive to keep God's Law because we are afraid that, if we do not, we will be harshly punished for failing to do so. This kind of fear is what a child has when being disciplined by a parent. The parent may be disciplining them to teach a lesson. The child, however, does not yet see the reason behind the punishment. All that is seen is the punishment itself and the pain it involves. This kind of fear is often prevalent in the early stages of our spiritual journey and perhaps never goes away entirely. No one enjoys the pain of punishment, even when we know we have brought that punishment upon ourselves. It is a kind of fear that must be

---

[1] For more on these various dimension of fear, see Josef Pieper, *Faith-Hope-Love* (San Francisco: Ignatius Press, 2012): 130-38.

purified by fire so that it can turn into something far greater.

Filial fear, by way of contrast, is sometimes called "chaste fear" and is the fear of sinning itself, because doing so is a way of dishonoring God. It is the love of a loyal son or daughter who does not wish to offend God, not out of fear of punishment, but because of our love for him and our deep desire to follow and be loyal to him. It is a fear of displeasing God because we love him and, despite our weakness, wish to show our love and respect for him by doing his will. It is a deeper, more authentic form of fear that tends to emerge in the later stages of our spiritual journey, even as its seed is planted in our hearts at the very outset. It is a fear of God born from our sense of being his adopted sons and daughters.

Mixed fear is an intermediate stage between *servile* and *filial fear*. As its name indicates, it represents a gradual shift from fear of punishment to fear of sinning, born of love for God himself. As its name also implies, it manifests itself in various forms of mixture. In some instances, *servile fear* is dominant. And in others, *filial fear* is more prevalent. The ideal is that, gradually over time, the *servile* element will decrease, and the *filial* element will increase. That is not to say that the reverse can never happen. It is, after all, possible for a person to backslide and allow the fear of punishment to dominate. The goal, however, is that one's relationship with Christ will deepen to such an extent that the fear of punishment will greatly diminish and hopefully one day entirely disappear.

Fear of the Lord is one of the seven gifts of the Holy Spirit and involves having a deep sense of awe before God's infinite majesty. We are overwhelmed by God's love for us and our call to share in his divine love for all eternity. As such, it is a perfection of the infused moral virtue of hope, for it deepens our focus on our ultimate end as we anticipate one day arriving there and can already taste it during our present earthly sojourn. It is also related to the infused moral virtue of temperance in that it seeks moderation in all things for the sake of the kingdom, which we have a deepened sense of already being in our midst. This kind of fear is closely related to the awe we experience when being in the presence of God. We take off our shoes and bow before his infinite majesty.[2]

---

[2] See Pinckaers, *The Sources of Christian Ethics,* 178-82.

We must remember that the various gifts of the Spirit are intimately related and that we receive them at Confirmation and grow at various rates as we deepen our relationship with Christ. When seen in this light, holiness is, first and foremost, a call to living a life in the Spirit, a life in which his various gifts and manifold fruits manifest themselves in our lives in very visible and concrete ways.

Life in the Spirit

As mentioned earlier, the indwelling of the Holy Spirit does not mean that the third Person of the Blessed Trinity actually makes his abode in the human heart. Rather, it states that his presence is felt by virtue of his nearness to us. Theologians sometimes use the image of the sun, which emits light and heat, to describe this divine indwelling. The closer the sun comes to us, the more its light and warmth are felt. If it gets too close, however, we would not be able to bear its closeness. Similarly, the more the Spirit influences our lives, the more we are influenced by his seven gifts and numerous gifts. These gifts and fruits, we might say, are to the Spirit what the light of the sun and the warmth it exudes are to the sun. While every analogy limps to some extent, this is a helpful way to distinguish the uncreated grace of the Spirit himself from the created graces (or, as the Christian East would have it, "energies") emanating from the Spirit. Let us now look at these numerous gifts and fruits.

According to the *Catechism of the Catholic Church,* there are seven *gifts of the Holy Spirit* (wisdom, understanding, counsel, knowledge, fortitude, piety, and fear of the Lord) and twelve *fruits* (charity, joy, peace, patience, kindness, goodness, generosity, gentleness, faithfulness, modesty, self-control, and chastity.[3] The gifts "...complete and perfect the virtues of those who receive them" and "make the faithful docile in readily obeying divine inspirations."[4] These supernatural sensitivities are given to us by God and are conferred upon us when we receive the sacrament of Confirmation. They embrace the various powers of the soul, both rational and sensual, build on the natural and infused theological and

---

[3] *Catechism of the Catholic Church*, nos. 1831-32.

[4] Ibid., no. 1831.

moral virtues, and give us an especially close sensitivity to the promptings of the Spirit. The fruits, in turn, "...are perfections that the Holy Spirit forms in us as the first fruits of eternal glory."[5] They point to the qualities of the citizens of heaven and are present, at least in seed form, to believers during their earthly sojourn as they make their way toward the heavenly Jerusalem.

Taken together, the gifts and fruits of the Spirit give us a taste of the life to come. They remind us that God wishes to befriend us and share his interior life with us, even now as we walk in faith to our heavenly homeland. They remind us that, even though we are "strangers in a foreign land" (*paroikia*), God has not abandoned us but has given us his Spirit to guide, protect, provide for, and comfort us as we make our way beyond the pale of death and live in the hope of one day seeing God face to face.

Prayer in the Spirit

---

[5] Ibid., 1832.

The Spirit is closer to us than we are to ourselves. He is always speaking to us, always moving us through his gentle promptings. He uses the light and warmth of his myriad gifts and fruits to stir our minds and hearts. He does so primarily through silence, the language of God. The problem for most of us is that our minds and hearts are so full of noise and the busyness of life that we do not sense his promptings, or, if we do, we generally ignore them as simply another passing thought or feeling that comes in one ear and out the other. The Spirit is constantly speaking to us. We see this in the prophet Elijah, who heard God's voice not in the whirlwind or earthquake or in the fire, but in a sheer silence, a still small voice, a small whispering sound (1Kgs 19:11-12). If we wish to listen to the movement of the Spirit in our hearts, we need to be still and know God for who he is: "Be still and know that I am God!" (Ps 46:10).

To hear the Spirit's voice, to listen to him and pray with him, we need above all to empty our minds and hearts of the noise of daily life and find a still centering point within us. It is there, in the stillness of our inner silence, that we will get in touch with the promptings of the Spirit. To empty ourselves in this way is already a movement of the Spirit in our lives, for he gives us the grace to purge ourselves of unnecessary distractions so we can focus on what truly matters. Only then will we sense the Spirit's promptings within us. As the Apostle Paul says, "Likewise the Spirit helps us in our weakness; for we do not know how to pray as we ought, but that very Spirit intercedes with sighs too deep for words. And God, who searches the heart, knows what the mind of the Spirit is, because the Spirit intercedes for the saints according to the will of God" (Rom 8:26-27). If we allow the Spirit to groan within us, if we listen to his promptings and let them move and lead us, we will be led by the Spirit from one moment to the next. As Paul says earlier in the same epistle: For all who the Spirit of God leads are children of God. For you did not receive a spirit of slavery to fall back into fear, but you have received a spirit of adoption. When we cry 'Abba! Father!' it is that very Spirit bearing witness with our spirit that we are children of God, and if children, then heirs, heirs of God and joint heirs with Christ—if, in fact, we suffer with him so that we may also be glorified with him" (Rom 8: 15-17).

Paul has put his finger on the pulse of the Spirit. He reminds us that the Spirit is not an inert concept or a vague idea, but a living reality, a Person who wishes to interact with and intercede for us. The Spirit is God's gift to us. As Jesus himself once remarked, he had to ascend to the Father so that he could send us his Spirit to protect, guide, and comfort us: "...I tell you the truth: it is to your advantage that I go away, for if I do not go away, the Advocate will not come to you; but if I go, I will send him to you" (Jn 16: 7). Jesus ascended to the Father so he could be present to us in a new and wonderful way. By sending his Spirit on Pentecost, he was able to dwell in the hearts of all his followers and lead them and the Church he founded from within.

The Practice of the Presence of God

Based on the Apostle Paul's insights, some theologians and spiritual writers have developed an approach to the spiritual life called "The Practice of the Presence of God." The seventeenth century Carmelite brother, Lawrence of the Resurrection (1614-91), the eighteenth-century Jesuit priest Jean-Pierre de

Caussade (1675-1751), and the eighteenth century Redemptorist founder, saint, and Doctor of the Church, Alphonsus de Liguori (1696-1787) have all provided insights into how one could live life by being immersed in the "Sacrament of the Present Moment."

Brother Lawrence does so in his *The Practice of the Presence of God*,[6] a collection of his letters and maxims published posthumously; De Caussade's letters to the Visitation Nuns in Nancy France were also published posthumously as *Abandonment to Divine Providence*;[7] while St. Alphonsus' approach to this practice was published in *The True Spouse of Jesus Christ* (1760-61),[8] a book addressed to nuns, but which he states has much value for all believers wishing to draw closer to the Lord. Each of these authors is worth reading, as each provides valuable insights

---

[6] Brother Lawrence, *The Practice of the Presence of God* (Gainesville, FL, Bridge-Logos Publishers, 1999).

[7] Jean-Pierre de Caussade, *Abandonment to Divine Providence*, trans. John Beevers (Garden City, NY: Image Books, 1975).

[8] Alphonsus de Liguori, *The True Spouse of Jesus Christ*, 16.3.

into how a person can let go of their personal agenda and sense the Spirit's promptings in the moment. Time and space, after all, are themselves creations of God, and God himself lives in Eternity beyond these boundaries and manifests himself most vividly in this world in the present moment. Since St. Alphonsus offers very concrete advice on this spiritual practice, we now look to his teaching for guidance.

Alphonsus tells us that the practice of the presence of God has three main effects: the avoidance of sin, the practice of virtue, and the union of the soul with God. He goes on to say that this practice can be done either with the intellect or the will. About the intellect, he states that we can: (1) imagine that Christ is with us, (2) behold him with the eyes of faith, (3) recognize him in his creatures, or (4) consider God within us. About the will, he says that we: (1) can frequently raise our hearts to God, (2) make the intention of pleasing God, or (3) quietly recollect ourselves with God. Each of these methods can be done either alone or together.[9] The goal here is to lift ourselves to God in prayer, either with our minds or hearts, and

[9] Ibid.

recognize that God is present both in our hearts and in our midst. What does this mean concretely?

We can, for example, imagine Jesus walking beside us as we take a walk in nature, or we can make an act of faith that he is there without imagining him, or we can sense the vestiges he has left of himself in creation, or we can sense his presence within us, since we have been created in his image and likeness. What is more, we can offer a heartfelt prayer to God, make an intention to please God in the present moment and throughout the day, or take some time out from our daily activities to recollect ourselves and be alone with God. In Alphonsus's mind, there is no one way to practice the presence of God. God is everywhere, and we can sense his presence in several ways.

Conclusion

Holiness is the call to become a friend of Jesus, the Son of God, who wishes to dwell in our hearts and we in his. He wants us to be one with him. Holiness is nothing other than living in an intimate relationship with God. A saint is someone who has fostered an intimate friendship with God to such an extent that we can say with the Apostle Paul, "I have been crucified with Christ, and it is no longer I who live, but it is Christ who lives in me" (Gal 2:19-20). For most of us, it takes a lifetime (and sometimes more) for us to get to the point of saying this with complete sincerity and heartfelt conviction. However long it takes, God is always ready to listen to us, accept us as we are, and walk with us as we make our way to our heavenly homeland.

Jesus tells us that we can best express our love for him by keeping his commandments. He narrowed the various laws of the Jewish Torah to two: love of God and love of neighbor. He went on to instruct us to love one another as he loves us. At the outset of our walk with the Lord, our motivations can be mixed and varied. Early on, we may do so out of fear of punishment. Later on, we may do so out of love for God. In the in-between time, we may have a mixture of these motivations. The lesson from all this is that no one ever stands still in the spiritual life. Either we are deepening our friendship with God or slowly distancing ourselves from him. God promises to walk with us on the road of sanctity. The choice, however, is ours to make. We can always decide to go our own way alone and without him.

To walk with God is to walk in the Spirit, who wants nothing more than to dwell within our hearts, and we to dwell in his. We know we are walking in the Spirit when we manifest in our lives his manifold gifts and fruits. When we walk in the Spirit, we allow him to groan within our hearts, comfort us, protect us, and intercede for us. He is our Advocate before God and, through him, Jesus unites us to his glorified humanity and brings us into the presence of his heavenly Father. The Spirit enables us to practice the presence of God in our daily lives. There are many ways we can do so, and we are free to follow one or many of the means outlined in this chapter. The important thing is to do so as best we can. When we practice the presence of God, we live in the sacrament of the present moment and become steeped in prayer. There are many ways of prayer, and this is the topic of our next chapter.

Our Befriending God

Do you believe that God calls everyone to be holy? Do you believe that he wants you to become a saint? If not, why not? Are you afraid of God? Are you afraid of the call to sanctity? How do you even view God? Do you fear him? If so, what kind of fear is it? Servile? Filial? Mixed? Have you ever experienced a deep awe of God's majesty? Have you ever experienced the Holy Spirit in your life? What does life in the Spirit mean to you? Have you ever tried to practice the Presence of God in your life? If so, what was it like? Have you ever thought about what it would be like always to sense God's presence?

Talking with God

Dear Lord, I sometimes find it hard to believe that you have called me to a life of holiness. I have so many faults and am wounded in so many ways. I try to do your will, but sometimes I fail miserably. I am sometimes afraid of punishment and at other times afraid of offending you out of love for you. Most of the time, it is a mixture of the two. I ask you to pour out your

Spirit upon me. Help me to live in the Spirit and pray in the Spirit. Help me to always sense your presence in me.

Chapter Four

The Ways of Prayer

Prayer, St. John Damascene (d. 749) tells us, "…is the raising of one's mind and heart to God or the requesting of good things from God."[1] It is about the relationship with the ground of our being and requires both faith in God and a heartfelt desire to share oneself with him. Because it requires faith and since faith is a gift from God, it is an action of both God and man. When we pray, God is already with us, helping us lift our minds and hearts to him. There are many forms of prayer, since we can express ourselves to God using words, gestures, music, song, art, or even silence. In this chapter, we will look at the various ways of prayer and explore what the Apostle Paul means when he asks us to "pray without ceasing" (1 Th 5:17).

---

[1] John Damascene, *On the Orthodox Faith*, 3.24; *Catechism of the Catholic Church*, no. 2559.

The Great Means of Salvation

Prayer, according to St. Alphonsus de Liguori, is the great means of salvation: "He who prays is certainly saved. He who prays not is certainly damned."[2] Those who do not pray will, in other words, spend eternity trying to fill a gaping hole in their souls with all sorts of things, pleasure, power, possessions, to name but a few,— but which can only be filled by God himself. God entered our world in the person of Jesus Christ to heal us from the wounds of sin and transform us from the inside out. Prayer is the primary means of achieving this goal. As a result of his paschal mystery, his passion, death, resurrection, and ascension into heaven,— he sent his Spirit to us, the members of his Body, to dwell within our hearts. As a result, we have easy and immediate access to our God, who is Transcendent, in the Person of the Father; Incarnate, in the Person of the Son; and Immanent, in the Person of the Spirit. The Holy Spirit is the Paraclete, our Advocate and Comforter. Because he

---

[2] Alphonsus de Liguori, *Prayer, The Great Means of Obtaining Salvation and All the Graces Which We Desire from God*, 1. concl.

dwells within us, we have easy and immediate access to the God of Love: "For all who the Spirit of God leads," the Apostle Paul reminds us, "are children of God" (Rom 8:14). As God's adopted sons and daughters, we can bring God all our needs, however great or small, and rest assured that, as a loving parent, he will respond in such a way that will secure our best interests. God, in other words, is always looking out for us and watches over us as a parent watches over a beloved son or daughter.

"Everyone," Alphonsus goes on to say, "receives sufficient grace to pray."[3] Since God wants everyone to be saved (1 Tm 2:4) and since, in Alphonsus's mind, God's grace is plentiful, prayer is not a difficult, esoteric action but something that is both agreeable and easy to do. In his work, *The Way to Converse Always and Familiarly with God*, he says that God wants us to disclose our hearts to him and speak to him with confidence and familiarity, as with a friend.[4] The problem is that many of us have a false image of God's true nature. As J. B. Philips once pointed out, our God

---

[3] Ibid., 201.

[4] Alphonsus de Liguori, *The Way to Converse Always and Familiarly with God*, 2.

is too small.[5] We have incorrect notions of who God is and act accordingly. Rather than seeing him as compassionate and loving, we often think of him as an angry God who watches our every move and who takes delight in punishing us for every careless mistake we make. Rather than turning to him when in need, we hide our secrets from him and mask ourselves when we pray, pretending to be someone we are not but whom we think would be acceptable in God's eyes.

God, of course, sees through our charades and is patient with us. He never forces himself but waits patiently for us to turn to him. As is often the case, this happens when we reach the end of our rope and have nowhere else to turn. It is at times like these that we can take off our masks and fully disclose ourselves to God. Intimacy, we are told, is a function of self-disclosure and loving attention.[6] God already knows our deepest needs and desires, but he wants to hear them from us. When we take the risk to share our

---

[5] J. B. Philips, *Your God Is Too Small* (New York: Macmillan, 1967), 7-9.

[6] Pat Collins, *Intimacy and the Hungers of the Heart* (Dublin: The /Columba Press, 1991), 104-22, 123-43.

innermost thoughts, desires, and needs with him, we can sense his Spirit comforting us deep down within, assuring us that, even if the worst possible scenario happens, "all shall be well," in the words of Julian of Norwich (c. 1343-c. 1416), for he is with us and will never abandon us.[7]

The Ways of Prayer

Prayer can be vocal, mental, or contemplative. Each of these ways of prayer has its own strengths and weaknesses. In this section, we shall look at each of them in turn and offer suggestions on how best to integrate them into our lives.

Vocal prayer is simply talking to God aloud. These words can either be set prayer forms, such as the Our Father, Hail Mary, and the Glory Be, or more spontaneous and from the heart. The great value of this way of prayer is that it exercises the body and, when said with reverence and deep internal piety, also both mind and spirit. Such prayer can be done either alone

---

[7] Julian of Norwich, *Showings (Long Text)*, chaps. 27, 32.

or in groups. It is also the form of prayer used in the Church's sacramental celebrations, especially the Eucharist. Such vocal prayer can also be done through music and song. St. Augustine is attributed with the saying, "To sing is to pray twice." Whether through song or simple unadulterated speech, vocal prayer has a unique way of raising our minds and thoughts to God. When prayed from the heart with sincerity, it engages the whole person and even the entire community. Its biggest weakness, however, is that the prayer (especially those that are set) can become repetitive and rote, and lose its meaning. As the saying goes, "Familiarity breeds contempt." If we are not careful, we can easily say these prayers without really meaning them. Just before he taught his disciples how to pray, he warned them, "When you are praying, do not heap up empty phrases as the Gentiles do; for they think that they will be heard because of their many words. Do not be like them, for your Father knows what you need before you ask him" (Mt 6:7). If we are not careful, even such beautiful prayers as the Our Father, Hail Mary, and Glory can become empty phrases which are said without heart and which, in effect, are not prayers at all, but hollow noise and babble.

Mental Prayer is simply talking to God in the quiet of our minds. There are times when talking to God aloud is not appropriate because of the circumstances. Even at such times, we can turn to God in prayer by retreating into our minds and hearts and speaking to him as one friend to another. Mental prayer is very important for our spiritual lives, so much so that, according to St. Alphonsus, it is morally necessary for our salvation.[8] That is to say that, without it, we would find it very difficult to find our way to God and secure a place in paradise. Louis Bouyer has pointed out that there are two basic approaches to mental prayer: the Jesuit, which uses silence and the imagination to raise one's heart and mind to God, and the Sulpician, which focuses on seeing Jesus before our eyes, then within our hearts, and finally in our hands.[9] St. Alphonsus wrote extensively on mental prayer and offers a very simple way

---

[8] Alphonsus de Liguori, *Mental Prayer and the Exercises of a Retreat*, 1.1.1-3.

[9] Louis Bouyer, *Introduction to the Spiritual Life* (Notre Dame, IN: Christian Classics, 2013), 110-14.

of opening our hearts to God. According to his mental prayer, it is meant to be permeated by silence. It has a preparatory period (or Introduction) in which we tell God we believe in him, ask him for mercy, and request light. It moves on to the main corpus (or Body), which involves reflecting on a mystery of the faith as it relates to our lives (Meditation), encourages us to express to God our feelings and affections regarding it (Affections), brings to God our various needs and wants (Petitions), and then asking him what he wants us to do regarding them (Resolution). The period of mental prayer then ends with a closing period (or Conclusion), where we thank God for the light received, ask him for the grace to carry out our resolution, and ask for the grace of perseverance.[10] Whatever approach to mental prayer we use, it is essential to our growth in the spiritual life.

Contemplation is wordless prayer. It allows the silence to permeate our souls. It does not need to say anything to God, because it knows that God is present deep within our hearts and dwells therein. "I

---

[10] Alphonsus de Liguori, *Mental Prayer and the Exercises of a Retreat*, 1.6.1-3.

look at him, and he looks at me." This is how the *Catechism of the Catholic Church* says what a simple peasant said to the Curé of Ars to describe how he prays before the Tabernacle.[11] Contemplation is a simple, silent gaze of faith. It can be acquired or infused. The former falls under the category of ascetical prayer. Here, grace is present, as it must be with all authentic Christian prayer, but we are still the primary persons praying. The Spirit assists us in our prayer. In the latter, however, the Spirit takes over and becomes the primary agent of prayer. This is pure mystical prayer. We cannot will this kind of prayer on our own; it is a pure gift of God. Vocal prayer, mental prayer, and acquired contemplation or recollection are the ascetical forms of prayer and represent the meat and potatoes of the spiritual life. They represent the kinds of prayer we can offer by cooperating with the Spirit's grace. Mystical prayer, however, is a pure gift of God and cannot be willed as the ascetical forms of prayer can. In her book *Interior Castle*, St. Teresa of Avila (1515-82) outlines the various states of mystical contemplation. They are: (1) infused

[11] *Catechism of the Catholic Church*, no. 2715.

contemplation, when the light of the Spirit enters our minds, (2) the prayer of quiet, when the Spirit inters our wills and gives us a deep sense of peace, (3) the prayer of union, when the Spirit enters of internal senses of memory and imagination and helps us see God's presence in our past and in our wildest imaginings, (4) the prayer of spiritual betrothal, when the Spirit pours into our external senses and gives us an experience of being outside ourselves in spiritual ecstasy, and (5) the prayer of spiritual marriage, when our souls are lifted into a close, intimate union with God and, while retaining our creaturely status, we experience ourselves as being completely one with him.[12]

It is important to remember that, when and if it occurs, mystical prayer is typically not long-lasting. That is why even the greatest mystics always return to the ascetical forms of prayer to maintain their relationship with the Lord in their daily lives. What is more, it is also important to remember that God wants us all to be saved and that we are all called to one day experience him face to face in the beatific

---

[12] See Teresa of Avila, *Interior Castle*, Mansions, 1-7.

vision. While most of us must wait for life after death to experience God in this way, he graces some individuals with this experience even in this life, encouraging us and giving us hope for something yet to come. When seen in this light, mystical prayer is a charismatic grace given not only to the individuals in question but also to build up the faith of the body of believers. We look to these mystics as a sign of hope for what we ourselves hope to experience one day in the life to come.

Pray without Ceasing

Having looked at the various forms of prayer, we can now delve into one of the most challenging and mysterious verses in all of Scripture. The Apostle Paul gives the Thessalonians the following exhortation: "rejoice always, pray without ceasing, give thanks in all circumstances; for this is the will of God in Christ Jesus for you" (1 Th 5:16-18). There have been several attempts in the Christian tradition to understand how we can "pray without ceasing," and we will look into these in turn. Before saying anything else, we should point out that to do so must be seen as God's will for us and that it is also intimately connected with the other two exhortations to rejoice always and to give constant thanks. Prayer, in other words, is not meant to be a burden but something that gives joy to the heart and enables us to see God's hand in all that happens to us. It is meant to be a thankful and joyous activity, one that fills the heart with a deep sense of the Spirit's presence in our lives and of the Spirit's ongoing love for us. Having said this, we can now ask ourselves, how has the phrase "pray without ceasing" been interpreted in the past? Down through history, there have been at least four interpretations of this enigmatic phrase: the Psalter, the Morning Offering, the Spirit's yearning and groaning within us, and the Prayer of the Heart. Let us look at each of these in turn.[13]

The Psalter refers to praying the 150 Psalms of the Old Testament in an ordered and cyclical manner throughout the day. Benedict of Nursia adopted this

---

[13] For an extended treatment of these four approaches to unceasing prayer, see Fabio Giardini, *Pray without Ceasing: Toward a Systematic Psychotheology of Christian Prayerlife* (Leominster, Herefordshire: Gracewing, 1998), 338-50.

ascetic practice of the early monks in the Rule he composed, which became the foundation of Western monasticism from the Middle Ages to the present day. It forms the basis of the *Liturgy of the Hours* (*Breviary*), which ordained priests and deacons of the Western Church are bound to recite five hours every day. The idea behind reciting these psalms and some choice New Testament hymns is to sanctify key points during the day, in the hope that they will overflow into the rest of the day. In the monastic tradition, these hours included: *Matins*, *Lauds, Prime, Terce, Sext*, *None*, *Vespers*, and *Compline*. The Psalms are heartfelt hymns that cover nearly every human emotion. It was thought that by chanting or, in the very least, reciting these psalms, we would be able to sanctify both day and night in giving glory and praise to the God of the universe.

The Morning Offering consists of making a specific intention at the beginning of the day to offer all one's works to God as a way of giving him adoration, glory, and praise. It has its roots in early Church theologians like Origen of Alexandria (c. 185-c. 253), who held that we could sanctify the day by making one specific intention at the outset of the day to offer all the good that we do to God. In this way, we can rest assured that, even though we may not be fully conscious or aware of God at every moment of the day, we know that we have focused all our efforts at the dawning of the day on finding a way to glorify the Lord through our words and actions. Since intention comprises one of the fundamental elements of the human act, we can rest easy in the knowledge that all the good we do will be oriented toward God. "Actions speak louder than words," the saying goes. This manner of prayer focuses not necessarily on being always aware of God (although that may happen at various points throughout the day), but on honoring him in the way we live our lives.

The Spirit's yearning within us reflects the Apostle Paul's depicting of the Spirit as our Advocate and Comforter who, "…helps us in our weakness; for we do not know how to pray as we ought, but that very Spirit intercedes with sighs too deep for words" (Rom 8:26). St. Augustine takes up this theme in his *Confessions*, where he says that the deep yearning we have for God is itself prayer: "…you have made us for yourself, and our hearts are restless until they can find rest in you."[14] Augustine recognizes that the Spirit yearning within our hearts makes us restless travelers who will not find peace until we see God at our journey's end. The yearning we experience in the present is but a foretaste of the heavenly banquet. It reminds us that we are wayfarers, strangers in a foreign land, with one foot in the City of Man and another in the City of God. The Spirit's presence in our hearts is a concrete sign of God's love for us and his promise that we will one day see him face to face in our heavenly homeland.

The Prayer of the Heart, also known as the Jesus Prayer, comes from the Eastern Christian tradition and involves the constant repetition of the words, "Lord Jesus Christ, Son of God, have mercy on me." We make these repetitions first with our tongues, then in sync with our breathing, and finally with the beating of our hearts. This is a gradual process that moves ever deeper into the heart, which is why it is called "The Prayer of the Heart": the words of the prayer are meant to keep our minds from distraction and allow our spirits to sing. This form of prayer is

[14] Augustine of Hippo, *Confessions*, 1.1.

rooted in the Eastern Orthodox book *The Philokalia* and became widely known through two nineteenth-century Eastern Orthodox works, *The Way of the Pilgrim* and *The Pilgrim Continues His Way*, which follow the wanderings of a Russian pilgrim as he seeks to discover the secrets of ceaseless prayer. It has since become popular throughout the Christian world and is one of the most popular Christian prayer forms today.

An Alternative Interpretation

Yet another way of understanding Paul's call to pray without ceasing is to look at it from the perspective of our human makeup.[15] From a Christian perspective, we are physical, psychological/intellectual, spiritual, and social beings. Paul himself pints this out in when he says: "May the God of peace himself sanctify you entirely; and may your spirit and soul and body be kept sound and blameless at the coming of

---

[15] For an extended treatment to thus approach to unceasing prayer, see Dennis J. Billy, *Evangelical Kernels: A Theological Spirituality of the Religious Life* (Staten Island, NY: Alba House, 167-84.

our Lord Jesus Christ" (1 Th 5:23). Here, he lists the three dimensions of human existence: spirit (*pneuma*), soul (*psyche*), and body (*soma*). Elsewhere, he brings out the fourth (social) dimension when he speaks of the body of Christ (*soma tou Christou*): "For just as the body is one and has many members, and all the members of the body, though many, are one body, so it is with Christ. For in the one Spirit we were all baptized into one body" (1 Cor 12:12-13). It bears noting that the Greek word for body (*soma*) differs from the word for flesh (*sarx*). While the former is a neutral term, the latter refers to the body under the influence of sin. The point being made here is that God wants us to express every dimension of our human makeup to him in prayer: the physical, the psychological/intellectual, the spiritual, and the social. What does this mean concretely?

First, we need to find ways of expressing the physical dimension of our being to the Lord. We can do this through vocal prayer, gestures, music, art, and the like. We also need to express our psychological and intellectual dimensions to the Lord through spiritual reading, *lectio divina*, mental prayer, and simply sharing with him our deepest feelings and emotions.

Next, we need to quiet ourselves, sit in silence with him, and allow our spirits to commune with him. We can do this by making a holy hour before the Blessed Sacrament, by praying before an icon, or by simply taking a walk in nature. Finally, we need to do this together. We are social beings and need each other throughout our spiritual journey. We can do this by attending a prayer meeting, reciting the rosary together, making a common novena, and in many other ways. Now, each of us will have a preference for how we relate to God. We need to acknowledge our strengths and be grateful for them. At the same time, we also need to confront our weaknesses. We need to ask ourselves what dimension of our human makeup we are not expressing to God and withholding from him. The challenge for each of us is to find the rhythm in our lives that helps us express every dimension of our human makeup to God. Since each of us is different, that daily, weekly, or monthly rhythm will be different from everyone else's. When we put them all together as members of Christ's body, however, they unite to offer a wonder polyphonic hymn of praise and Glory to the Triune God, our Creator, Redeemer, and Sanctifier.

The beautiful thing about all this is that it all comes together when we celebrate the Liturgy. When we gather for the Eucharist, "the source and summit of the Christian life," we engage the senses through processions, music, song, gestures, liturgical art, colorful vestments, burning candles, incense, and other elements. We also nurture the psychological/intellectual dimensions of our lives when we read from Scripture, break open God's Word, and, through the homily, seek to touch both mind and heart. When celebrated well, the Liturgy also has moments of silence, usually after the homily or Communion, when those gathered can sit in silence and allow the Spirit to hover over them in peace. Finally, we do this together, as the People of God who, as strangers in a foreign land, have banded together with Christ, our Lord, as our head, to get a little bit closer on this particular day of our lives toward our heavenly homeland. What is beautiful about this interpretation of what it means to pray without ceasing is that it highlights the intimate connection between personal and liturgical prayer. Personal prayer, in other words, leads us to Liturgy and vice versa.

Conclusion

What can we say by way of conclusion? Prayer requires faith and is, therefore, an activity that involves both God and us. Everyone receives sufficient grace to pray. Prayer, in turn, is "the great means of salvation." "If you pray, you will be saved; if you do not, you will be damned." If we do not pray, we will spend the rest of eternity trying to fill a gaping hole within our souls with everything else but God, the only Person who could fill it. Prayer is the means by which we can foster an intimate friendship with God. Paradise for God, after all, is the human heart.

There are many forms of prayer: ascetical and mystical; vocal, mental, and contemplative. Ascetical prayer is the meat and potatoes of the spiritual life. It is something each of us can do at any time in our lives with the help of God's grace. Mystical prayer, by way of contrast, is a pure gift from God. It differs from ascetical prayer in that it is not something that we ourselves can choose to do. Through it, the Holy Spirit becomes the primary agent of prayer, while we, all the while, maintain our individuality and creaturely status. We are all called to the mystical life. For most of us, however, the beatific vision awaits us once our sojourn in life comes to an end. In the present life, however, God gives mystical experiences to certain individuals to strengthen believers' faith and to foreshadow things to come.

There have been several interpretations of St. Paul's exhortation to the Thessalonians to pray without ceasing: the Psalter, the Morning Offering, the Spirit yearning within us, the Prayer of the Heart. An alternative interpretation looks at the various dimensions of our human makeup, the physical, psychological/intellectual, spiritual, and social, and to find that particular rhythm in our lives that will express each of these to God in a way unique to each of us. We need to acknowledge which of these dimensions we prefer, as well as which we overlook and perhaps even ignore. God wants to befriend us on every level of our human makeup. For this reason, it is up to each of us to find a way of expressing each of these dimensions to him in a way particular to our circumstances. It is also important for us to see that, when we come together for Eucharist, we express each of these dimensions of our human makeup to God. When we go forth at the end of Mass, we leave strengthened in each of these dimensions to continue our following of Christ.

Our Befriending God

Do you believe that prayer is the "Great Means of Salvation"? Do you believe that we are called to pray without ceasing? How do you pray? Do you understand the various ways of prayer? Which way do you prefer? Which way would you consider your strengths? Which do you need to work on? Do you believe that we must offer prayers to God using every dimension of our human makeup? Which do you prefer? Which ones have you neglected? Have you ever tried any of the ways listed in this chapter for practicing the presence of God? If not, why not? If so, which ones? Have you found the particular rhythm of prayer that best suits you at this point in your life? Are you willing to explore the various ways of prayer?

Talking with God

Dear Lord, at times I find myself saying with the disciples, "Lord, teach us to pray?" (Lk 11:1). I pray your prayer, "The Lord's Prayer," many times each day, but too often find myself just mouthing the words without putting my heart and soul into them. I understand that I can relate to you in many ways and ask you to find the way especially suited to me. Is it a vocal prayer? mental prayer? Simply resting with you in the quiet of my soul? Any mixture of these? Help me, Lord, help me. Help me to live in your presence at all times.

Chapter Five

Following the Call

Prayer takes the wax out of our spiritual ears and enables us to hear the voice of God more clearly. Hearing that voice, however, is only part of our journey to holiness. We also need to follow it.

We need to listen to that still small voice within our hearts and allow it to lead us through the day's events. The challenge before each of us is to do just that. We need to empty ourselves of the useless noise and banter that fill our minds and allow silence to fill them. Silence, we have seen, is the language of God. We need to befriend the surrounding silence to hear what the Lord is saying to us.

The plain truth of the matter is that we need God's grace even to do that. Without his help, we will never be able to listen to the voice of his Spirit and respond to his promptings. Before we do anything else, we need to ask God to help us listen to him and follow the Spirit's lead.

Hearing the Voice

The Spirit is constantly speaking to us, not so much through words as through the silence deep within our hearts, which enables us to sense his promptings. To be led by the Spirit means being able to empty ourselves of all the disquiet and busyness in our minds and hearts and to rest in the stillness deep within our hearts. To hear the Spirit's voice, we must befriend this stillness and allow it to move us out of ourselves and rest in it. We also need to be able to distinguish between the ways of the Spirit and those of the Evil One, who, as a master of deceit and father of lies, is always trying to fool us into following what he disguises as truth.

The Apostle Paul gives us a trustworthy way of telling whether something comes from the Spirit or the Evil One. The desires of the flesh, he says, are opposed to those of the Spirit (Gal 5:17). He goes on to list the works of the flesh and contrasts them with those of the Spirit:

> Now the works of the flesh are obvious: fornication, impurity, licentiousness, idolatry,

> sorcery, enmities, strife, jealousy, anger, quarrels, dissensions, factions, envy, drunkenness, carousing, and things like these...By contrast, the fruit of the Spirit is love, joy, peace, patience, kindness, generosity, faithfulness, gentleness, and self-control. There is no law against such things (Gal 5:19-23).

The Spirit wants us to be free and to become our truest, deepest selves. The Evil One, by way of contrast, wants to control us like puppets on a string. He tries his best to darken our minds and hearts and tempts us into thinking we are better than we really are. The Spirit teaches humility, while the Evil One teaches pride. He tempts us to place ourselves at the center of the moral universe and to have the power to decide what is right and wrong. He wants us to put ourselves aside and take God's place, tricking us into thinking we are more important than we really are. The story of the Fall in chapter three of Genesis reveals the extent of the Evil One's lies and the consequences that followed for humanity. The tragedy of the Fall is that by eating the forbidden fruit, Adam and Eve did not become like gods but were stripped of preternatural gifts and cast out of Paradise.

Hearing the voice of the Spirit requires humility, patience, and prayer. We need to accept the truth about ourselves and recognize that our propensity toward sin is one of the consequences of the Fall. We also need to be patient with ourselves and recognize that we cannot keep God's Law without his help and that our journey to holiness will be long and arduous. Most of all, we need to fall on our knees and ask God for the grace to hear the Spirit's voice deep within our hearts. Left to ourselves, we would wander through life without direction or purpose. God entered our world in the Person of Jesus Christ to show us the way to the Father. By conquering death through his passion, death, and resurrection, he has opened the gates of heaven and given us his Spirit to accompany us on our journey home. We hear the Spirit's voice when we empty ourselves of our undue creaturely attachments, rest in the stillness within us, and respond with gratitude to his myriad gifts and fruits.

Acknowledging the Call

God speaks to us through signs. As the saying goes, "Jesus Christ is the sacrament of God. The Church is the sacrament of Christ. The sacraments are those of the Church." Sacraments are external signs given to us by Christ to mediate grace. Jesus speaks to us through the Church and her sacraments. They are actions of Christ that tell us he is "Emmanuel, God with us" and that accompany us throughout our lives. The Eucharist, we have seen, is "the source and summit of the Christian life." It differs from the other sacraments in that it is not only an action of Christ but Christ himself. He entered our world not only some 2,000 years ago, but also every time we celebrate the Eucharist. There he immerses us in his passion, death, and resurrection, and turns bread and wine into his Body and Blood. He gives us himself to eat and drink so that he can be our very food and nourishment and become one with us in Holy Communion. Receiving Holy Communion is, at the same time, both personal and communal. Because he is infinite, God can treat each of us as if we were the only person in existence. At the same time, when we receive him at Eucharist, our identity as members of his Mystical Body, the Church, is also proclaimed. When we receive Holy Communion, we share more deeply in Jesus' glorified humanity and go with him into the presence of the Father.

Jesus uses the Church, the Scriptures, and the sacraments to call each of us by name: "My sheep hear my voice. I know them, and they follow me. I give them eternal life, and they will never perish. No one will snatch them out of my hand. What my Father has given me is greater than all else, and no one can snatch it out of the Father's hand. The Father and I are one" (Jn 10:27-30). What the prophet Isaiah said of the people of Israel now applies to the Church, the New Israel: "But now thus says the Lord, he who created you, O Jacob, he who formed you, O Israel: Do not fear, for I have redeemed you; I have called you by name, you are mine" (Is 43:1). We hear the voice of the Lord when we experience the fruits of the Spirit in our lives. We hear the voice of the Lord when we hear the Word of God proclaimed. We hear the Lord's voice when the Church teaches. We hear his voice when we receive the sacraments. Jesus is "Emmanuel, God with us." He knows his sheep, and they know him. When we hear his voice, we must acknowledge the call and follow him. When we do so, we must trust that he is leading us to green pastures. In the words of the Psalmist: "The Lord is my shepherd, I shall not want. He makes me lie down in green pastures; he leads me beside still waters; he restores my soul. He leads me in the right paths for his name's sake. Even though I walk through the darkest valley, I fear no evil; for you are with me; your rod and staff they comfort me" (Ps 23:1-4). Jesus calls us by name, asks us to put aside our fears, and follow him. Jesus loves us with a love so perfect that he was willing to lay down his life for his sheep. He wants us to trust him and follow him wherever he goes.

Every Sunday, Solemnity, and major feast day, we gather for Eucharist and acknowledge what we believe by reciting the Creed. This profession of faith is an acknowledgment of the main precepts of the Catholic faith. We should not take these words lightly. Many of our ancestors in the faith held them close to their hearts and were willing to die for them. To recite the Creed with deep faith and conviction is the mark of a true believer. When we say those words, we need to confront ourselves and honestly ask whether we truly take them to heart. Are we willing to die for them? As the old saying goes, "If you were on trial for being a Christian, would there be enough evidence to convict you?" If we do not acknowledge Christ through our words and actions, will he acknowledge us when he comes again in glory? Listen to what Jesus says: "Not everyone who says to me, 'Lord, Lord,' will enter the kingdom of heaven, but only the one who does the will of my Father in heaven. On that day, many will say to me, 'Lord, Lord, did we not prophesy in your name, and cast out demons in your name, and do many deeds of power in your name?' Then I will declare to them, 'I never knew you; go away from me, you evildoers'" (Mt 7:21-23).

Following Jesus

In the movie, *Full of Grace* (2015), which takes place about ten years after Christ's resurrection, at the time when his mother is about to finish her earthly sojourn, Mary responds to Peter, when he shares with her the great difficulty he is experiencing in leading the nascent Church, by saying, "He never asked you to lead. He only asked you to follow." Following

Christ means being willing to go into the dark, lonely, and violent places of this forlorn, sinful world, to preach a message of hope in God's redemptive love. We follow Christ because we have a personal relationship with him. He has befriended us and now dwells within us by the power of his Spirit: "For 'In him we live and move and have our being'" (Acts 17: 28). With the Apostle Paul, we acclaim: "…it is no longer I who live, but it is Christ who lives in me. And the life I now live in the flesh I live by faith in the Son of God, who love m and gave himself for me" (Gal 2:20). Christ shows his love for us, and his followers seek to love him in return. We do so, not on our own power, but through the power of the Spirit who lives in our hearts and empowers us to follow in his footsteps.

We live not by the world's values but by those of Jesus our Lord. In his book, *Your God Is Too Small,* J. B. Phillips brings out the stark contrast between these two world views:

Most people think:

Happy are the pushers, for they get on in the world.
Happy are the hard-boiled, for they never let life hurt them.
Happy are they who complain, for they get their own way in the end.
Happy are the blazé: for they never worry over their sins.
Happy are the slave-drivers, for they get results.
Happy are the knowledgeable men of the world, for they know their way around.
Happy are the trouble-makers, for people have to take notice of them.

Jesus Christ said:

Happy are those who realize their spiritual poverty; they have already entered the kingdom of Reality.
Happy are they who bear their share of the world's pain: in the long run, they will

know more happiness than those who avoid it.

Happy are those who accept life and their own limitations: they will find more in life than anybody.

Happy are those who long to be truly "good": they will fully realize their ambition.

Happy are those who are ready to make allowances and to forgive: they will know the love of God.

Happy are those who are real in their thoughts and feelings: in the end, they will see the ultimate Reality, God.

Happy are those who help others to live together: they will be known as doing God's work.[1]

We are a people of the Beatitudes (Mt. 5:3-11). Jesus lived by values that were the opposite of the world's. The citizens of God's kingdom are poor in spirit, mourners, meek, people who long for righteousness, merciful, pure in heart, peacemakers, and

---

[1] Phillips, *Your God Is too Small*, 92-93.

willing to suffer for righteousness. When Jesus shares the beatitudes, he is talking about himself. He is first and foremost, a citizen of God's kingdom. He invites his followers to follow him in leading a life of virtue that points to a kingdom that is not of this world but of one still to come, yet already present in the hearts of his disciples.

We follow Jesus because he is leading us to his Father in heaven. He became man so that we might be immersed in his paschal mystery, share in his glorified humanity, and enter with him into the presence of the Father. God loves us so much that he wishes us to share in his creative, redemptive, and sanctifying actions. As members of Christ's Mystical Body and filled with his Spirit, we join him in the establishment of a New Creation, one that redeems the old, sanctifies it, and, in doing so, transforms it into something continuous with what it was yet more than, without Christ and his Spirit, it could never have even dreamed of one day becoming. In becoming man, Christ has allowed us to become "friends of God," saints who walk with him along the path of holiness toward our heavenly homeland into the presence of the Father. There, we share in the intimate love of the

Blessed Trinity, Father, Son, and Spirit, the God of Love from whom all things have come to be and continue to be, the God who has created us in his image and likeness so we could enter into relationship with him and love him with the freedom of his adopted sons and daughters. Jesus, "the way, the truth, and the life" (Jn 14:6), has revealed this mysterious God of Love to us as the truth, the source of all life, and the way to our final destiny.

Our Saintly Mother

Mary, the mother of Jesus and our mother, was Jesus' first and closest disciple. She was "full of grace" and responded to the Spirit's promptings throughout her entire life. Catholics worship God alone (latria) yet venerate her with special reverence (hyperdulia) because of her unique role in the mystery of our redemption. She is a "friend of God, a "woman of the beatitudes," and presently sits at her Son's right hand as Queen of the Universe. We have given her many titles: Second Eve, Queen of Peace, Seat of Wisdom, Mirror of Justice, Help of Christians, Health of the Sick, Refuge of Sinners, to name but a few, because of her invaluable role in her Son's (and our) earthly sojourn. Because of Jesus and our closeness to him, we have become her adopted sons and daughters. We know this because Jesus gave her to us as his parting gift when he said to her, "Woman, here is your son," and to the beloved disciple, "Here is your mother" (Jn 19:26-27). Just as the beloved disciple took her into his own home at that moment, so are we asked to take her into the home of our hearts. Mary, in turn, has now become our mother, who cares for us, watches over us, and intercedes for us.

Mary looks upon us as she looks upon her Son. He has befriended us, and she wishes to befriend us as well. In caring for us and watching over us, her only desire is to draw us closer to her Son. As with any authentic friendship, this means actively looking out for one's friends' well-being. This is especially true if, in addition to being a friend, one also considers us a beloved son or daughter. Mary accompanied her Son from the very first moment of his existence in her womb, to his birth in Bethlehem, to his flight to Egypt, to his hidden life in Nazareth, throughout his public ministry, to his entrance to Jerusalem, to his death on the cross, and beyond. Just as Jesus accompanies us throughout our lives, so does she, like him and because of him, walk before us to guide us, behind us to catch us when we fall, beside us to accompany us on our journey, and live within us to befriend us and give us a sense of warmth and belonging. She goes wherever her Son goes, bringing with her a mother's loving care and concern.

Because Mary is Jesus' first and closest follower, she has his ear. We see this most clearly at the wedding of Cana (Jn 2:1-12), when she tells him that the wedding party has run out of wine, and he turns the water in six stone water jars into wine, even though he told her that his hour had not yet come. Similarly, she looks at our various needs and wants (especially at our need for conversion) and asks her Son to bless us with the grace to repent of our sins, change our lives, and follow him more closely. As the fathers of the Second Vatican Council remind us, she "is invoked in the Church under the titles of Advocate, Helper, Benefactress, and Mediatrix."[2] She is our saintly mother who constantly prays and intercedes for us to her Son. She is Our Mother of Perpetual

---

[2] Second Vatican Council, *Lumen gentium*, no. 62.

Help, someone who looks upon us as she looks upon her Son and who never takes her eyes off us.

Conclusion

Jesus once said, "If any want to become my followers, let them deny themselves and take up their cross daily and follow me" (Lk 9:23). The call to discipleship involves hearing the Lord's voice within our hearts, recognizing it as his voice, acknowledging it, and then following it. Just as the good shepherd is willing to lay down his life for his sheep, as Jesus' disciples we are called to lay down our lives for him and for the love of his people. Except Judas, who betrayed him, and the beloved disciple, who lived to a ripe old age, all of the other apostles suffered a martyr's death. They did so because they knew in their minds and hearts that Jesus had truly risen from the dead and that one historical fact changed everything.

C.S. Lewis once wrote: "A man who was merely a man and said the sort of things Jesus said would not be a great moral teacher. He would either be a lunatic at a level with the man who says he is a poached egg, or else he would be the Devil of Hell. You must make your choice. Either this man was, and is, the Son of God: or else a madman or something worse."[3] The apostles James and John, two brothers whom Jesus nicknamed *Boanerges* ("The Sons of Thunder") followed Christ and gave their lives up for him in two distinct ways. James shed his bled for Christ in a "red martyrdom." John, in turn, gave his life up for him by living a holy life in a "white martyrdom." When we understand that the word, "martyr," means "witness," it becomes clear that Christ himself, who testified to the Father's love for all humanity, is the "red martyr" par excellence, and Mary, his mother, whose heart was pierced by a sword at the foot of the cross, is the "white martyr" par excellence. What is more, in his encyclical *Veritatis Splendor*, John Paul II says that living the moral life in today's world is a type of martyrdom.[4] That is to say that living a life of virtue and giving oneself to the inviolability of the moral order, even to the point of being willing to shed one's blood for it, is a true mark of Christian witness. These insights challenge us to examine our lives and ask

---

[3] C.S. Lewis, *Mere Christianity* (New York: Macmillan, 1969), 55-56.

[4] John Paul II, *Veritatis splendor*, no. 93.

ourselves what kind of Christians we are. Let us also remember the words of Jesus in the Book of Revelation, "I wish that you were either hot or cold. So, because you are lukewarm, and neither hot nor cold, I am about to spit you out of my mouth" (Rv 3:15-16).

A true and authentic following of Christ requires us to be one with his Spirit. Jesus himself once said, I came to bring fire to the earth, and how I wish it were already kindled!" (Lk 12:49). It is no mistake that the Holy Spirit manifested himself at Pentecost, the birthday of the Church, in the form of tongues of fire (Acts 2:3). It is also important to remember that Mary herself was in the upper room on that day and continues to accompany the Church in her mission to spread the Gospel message to the ends of the earth. As we close this chapter, let us ask ourselves what our role is in spreading this Good News. God has a plan for each of us. It remains for us to listen to his voice, acknowledge it, embrace it, and follow it wherever it leads.

Our Befriending God

Have you ever felt as though God were speaking to you? If so, what were the surrounding circumstances of this experience? How did it make you feel? Did you feel challenged? Afraid? At peace? Did you acknowledge his voice? If so, how did you do so? What was he asking of you? Was it something general or specific? How did you respond to this call? Do you believe that God speaks to you constantly through the promptings of His Spirit? What must you do to be more in touch with these promptings? Have you emptied your heart so God's Spirit can touch you there and even dwell there?

Talking with God

Dear Lord, there are times when I feel close to you and other times when you seem very distant. I believe that you love me despite the many times I have turned away from you and have refused to listen to the promptings of your Spirit. Help me to live in constant communion with you. Help me not only to listen, but also to acknowledge and respond to that still small voice within my soul. I love you, Lord. Help me to follow you without ever counting the cost.

Conclusion

Saints are "friends of God." This is how they were referred to in the early Church, and this meaning holds to this day. God calls us all to an intimate friendship with him and to live in holiness. There are, of course, different levels of friendship. A canonized saint is someone whom the Church has identified as having already made their way to God and enjoying an intimate relationship with him. Most of us, however, are still on the journey home along the threefold way of purgation, illumination, and union. We are "saints in the making," so to speak, people in relationship with God, but with still a long way to go before we are ready to see him face to face. Those of us in this situation live in the hope that our friendship with God will continue to deepen in this life and the next to such an extent that we will one day see him face to face and be with him for all eternity. Such is the call of holiness.

The Catholic vision of life states that we are all "strangers in a foreign land" (*paroikia*). We are on a journey to our heavenly homeland with one foot in the City of Man and the other in the City of God. This journey is part and parcel of this call to sanctity. Just as Jesus entered our world to become one of us (in the mystery of the Incarnation), gave himself to us completely to the point of dying for us (in the mystery of his Passion and Death), became nourishment for us (in the mystery of the Eucharist), and a source of hope for us (in the mystery of his Resurrection), so too are we called to do the same by entering the worlds of those around us, giving ourselves to them, becoming nourishment, and a source of hope for them. We can do this only with the help of God's Spirit living within our hearts. Prayer, both liturgical and personal, is the great means of salvation: if we pray, we will be saved; if we do not, we will be lost. Prayer is a way of ensuring we are rooted in the Spirit, able to hear his quiet voice deep within our hearts, acknowledge his presence in our lives, and respond to his promptings. When seen in this light, a saint is a person rooted in the Spirit who recognizes his promptings, acknowledges them, and responds accordingly.

The call to holiness is just that,—a call. This book has been about helping us to listen to the Lord's voice, the Good Shepherd's voice, when he calls. The Lord's always speaking to us through sacramental signs instituted by Christ to give grace. Jesus is the sacrament of God; the Church, the sacrament of Christ; the seven sacraments, sacraments of the Church. Jesus speaks to us through these signs and accompanies us throughout our lives. He also speaks to us in the circumstances of our lives, and when we converse with him, heart to heart, as with a friend. The problem for many of us is that our minds and hearts are filled with the noise of so many worldly attractions that we find it difficult to hear his voice. Let us never sell God short. He wants to befriend us and is, in this very moment, actively seeking our well-being. He is constantly searching for us, calling each of us by name, and never relents. So let us heed the words of Jesus when he says, "Let any with ears listen!" (Mt 11:15). Let us listen and respond. Let us take up the crosses he has asked us to bear. Let us take them up each day and follow him.

www.ingramcontent.com/pod-product-compliance
Lightning Source LLC
LaVergne TN
LVHW040223110826
845146LV00004B/1267

* 9 7 9 8 8 8 8 7 0 5 4 2 1 *